STEPFAMILIES

© Aladdin Books 1990

First published in the United States in 1990 by
Gloucester Press, 387 Park Avenue South, New York NY 10016

Printed in Belgium   All rights reserved

Design: Andy Wilkinson, Rob Hillier
Editor: Catherine Bradley
Picture research: Cecilia Weston-Baker
Illustrator: Ron Hayward Associates
Consultant: Pete Sanders

The publishers would like to acknowledge that the photographs
reproduced in this book have been posed by models or have
been obtained from photographic agencies.

Library of Congress Cataloging-in-Publication Data

Grunsell, Angela.
    Stepfamilies / Angela Grunsell.
        p. cm. -- (Let's talk about)
    Summary: Discusses what happens to children when their
parents remarry.
    ISBN 0-531-17244-9
    1. Stepfamilies--United States--Juvenile literature. 2.
Stepchildren--United States--Psychology--Juvenile literature.
[1. Stepchildren. 2. Stepfamilies.] I.Title. II. Title: Stepfamilies.
HQ759.92.G78 1990
306.874--dc20
                                        90-3219   CIP   AC

"LET'S TALK ABOUT"

STEPFAMILIES

ANGELA GRUNSELL

Gloucester Press
London · New York · Toronto · Sydney

"Why talk about stepfamilies?"

People don't talk about stepfamilies very much. There isn't a television program called *Stepfamily Fortunes*. Advertisements don't show us stepmothers talking about how to get the stains out of their stepson's football shirts. But, by the year 2001, more children may live in stepfamilies than in any other kind of family. Already a very large number of adults and children live as members of stepfamilies. This is partly because more people do not choose to stay with the same partner for life, as they used to years ago.

We need to talk about stepfamilies because they are one of the most normal ways that children and adults live together. This book will help you to think about stepfamilies – maybe yours or other people's.

Some of these children working together at school are likely to live in stepfamilies.

"What is a stepfamily?"

A stepfamily is made, not born. The words stepmother and stepfather came about because the new partner "steps in" to help raise the children, and keep a home going with one of the children's parents.

A stepfamily is made when two adults get together and one or both already have children. The children may be young or grown up. The stepfamily may live together all the time, only some of the time, or not at all. For example, some children visit the parent they don't live with at weekends or for holidays.

Jean is Nico and Sonia's mother and Hamid is their stepfather. Their father, Chris, lives with Marie and her children, Ahmed and Sunita. They are Nico and Sonia's stepbrother and sister.

6

Marie   Chris   Jean   Hamid

Sunita   Ahmed   Sonia   Nico

"How are stepfamilies made?"

Stepfamilies can be formed in several different ways. They are often created after a separation or divorce. Couples may separate when they are not getting along. Couples end their marriage when they get divorced. Sometimes stepfamilies come about after the death of one parent. A widow or widower marries a new partner, who becomes a stepparent to her or his children. Also, a mother who has always been a single parent may decide to live with or marry a lover who then becomes her children's stepparent.

Someone who acts as a stepparent may be the same sex as the child's parent, but more often they are of the opposite sex. They may live alone together or with other adults and children. The children in a stepfamily often remember living with other adults in the past, but not always. Sometimes a stepfamily is formed just before or after a child is born, and is the only family the child has ever known.

Stepfamilies often have many relatives. Outings with all the members of the stepfamily can become a very large group.

"What makes a stepfamily different?"

Of course children do not choose their parents – their parents choose each other. When your parents decided to have you they may have been in a long-term partnership or they may have only been close to each other for a short time. Most adults feel they need another adult to share their thoughts and feelings with, either as a lover or as a friend.

The main thing that is different about being a child in a stepfamily is that the two adults you live with chose each other after you were born rather than before. You may still see the parent who is not part of the stepfamily you live with. That parent and your stepparent may have her or his new family, which includes stepbrothers and sisters.

Dionne and her sister live with their mother and stepfather. But they visit their father and their new stepbrothers at the weekend.

"Why did Dad have to change everything?"

Sometimes the parents or children in a stepfamily feel unable to live in the present and enjoy it. They may long for the way things used to be before they became part of a stepfamily.

Many stepfamilies are formed after loss or separation from a parent that the children can remember. When a big change like this happens in people's lives, they need to mourn what they have lost. Sometimes a stepparent joins the family soon after a parent has moved out. Feelings of loss when this happens can stay with the children and adults for a long time. These feelings can get tangled up with the new relationship that is just beginning.

"When my dad left mom and me, he moved in with Gloria and her son. I was very angry with him for messing up our family. Now I miss him."

It's important to have time with your own parent and share a particular activity.

"Sometimes I feel left out of our new family. Is there anything I can do?"

In families of all kinds, everyone wants and needs their share of time for attention and love. Sometimes a stepparent joins a parent and child who have been living alone together. The child may have less time alone with her or his parent than before. The adults may have jokes and secrets between themselves. The adults may kiss and cuddle or have arguments when the child is in the same room.

Sometimes the parent and child leave the stepparent out of their familiar games and habits. Georgio's stepmother said she often felt ignored when Georgio and his father Marco would talk with each other alone. She found it difficult to say she wanted time on her own with Marco. She started slamming the doors when Georgio stayed up after 8 pm. In the end they talked about it and worked out a solution. Marco now goes out with Georgio on Tuesday evenings and on other weekdays Georgio goes to his room at 8 pm.

"I like my stepmother. Why are stepmothers always bad in storybooks?"

There are lots of wicked stepparents, stepsisters and stepbrothers in fairy tales. The story of Cinderella shows someone who is still mourning the loss of her mother and unhappy because she is being treated badly by her stepmother and stepsisters. Most of these stories are very old. When they were first being told, many parents of young children died early in life from diseases we can now cure. Fathers died of battle wounds and accidents. Mothers died when they were giving birth. These stories tell of hard lives when people did not have many choices. Widows with children married men with children to escape being poor.

In Hansel and Gretel the father and stepmother did not have enough food for the family, but the children overcame this and found lots of money.

"Are there problems in stepfamilies?"

Fairy tales concentrate all the uncomfortable and destructive feelings that various family members sometimes have toward each other into one person. That person is the newcomer, the stepparent. But every story has two sides to it. How might Cinderella's stepmother have talked about Cinderella to a friend? It may be easier to think that you were not the cause of an argument between you and someone else in your family. But it is seldom true that misunderstandings come down to one person. Real people are a mixture of good and bad feelings and actions. Children and adults can sometimes act unreasonably.

Couples often need special times together just as parents and children do. Recognizing other people's rights and needs is something we all have to learn to do whatever kind of family we are in.

"Does living with a stepparent mean my life will change?"

When children become part of a stepfamily they may have to move to join a new partner. Sometimes the stepparent moves into the house where the children are already living. When members of two families start to live together none of them will be living exactly as they did before. Each person will have to adapt to the living habits of the others. A stepparent will have likes and dislikes about food and television programs just as a child does. Things may change that used to be fixed, like the times of meals. It takes time for families to work out the best ways to live together.

> Grandparents have often lived through many big changes in their own lives. It can be interesting to ask them about those changes and how they coped with them.

"Do I have to love everyone in my stepfamily?"

Nobody has to love another person. Sometimes stepparents and stepchildren come to care deeply about each other and sometimes they don't. Sometimes they get to like each other and become good friends and sometimes they never get to know each other really well at all.

Love between people grows from doing things together and sharing special times. It can grow from the trust and closeness you feel when someone has cared for you if you are ill or unhappy. But there is nothing automatic about it.

Although two adults may "fall in love" very suddenly with each other, the love between adults and children who live together usually takes a lot longer to grow.

"I see my father and my stepmother every other weekend. I know both my mother and my father love me. I like my stepmother. She's a lot of fun."

"Can there be one big happy family?"

Since so many people live in stepfamilies, lots of adults and children have stepbrothers and stepsisters. Children don't choose their stepsisters and stepbrothers any more than they choose their own sisters and brothers.

Although they may only live together some of the time, or be very different ages and lead very separate lives, they have parents and stepparents in common. This means they are likely to meet at family celebrations and funerals, as well as when they visit relatives. Children don't necessarily love or like their stepsisters or stepbrothers. They may find their habits and ways of behaving very annoying. But sometimes they get along very well and are close throughout their lives.

Lisa and Joyce share an interest in fashion and sports. They have plenty to talk about when they are together at weekends.

Getting along with a stepbrother may not be easy. Jealousy can be a problem within any family, especially when it seems he always gets what he wants.

"Why do I have to miss the school football matches?"

George likes football. He was picked for his school team and stays after school for football practice. When there are matches they are always on Saturday mornings when he is at his dad's house. He goes to a music club on Saturday mornings with his stepsister Marina, which he enjoys. But recently he has been feeling he would like to be able to make a choice about whether he plays football or goes to his dad's. He is finding it difficult to tell his friends why he can't ever play in the football matches, although he knows the coach understands. Sometimes they tease him and say he's chicken. He hasn't told his dad because he doesn't know how to tell him about this, or what he should ask for.

What would you do? Is there any advice you could give George? Who could George talk to about this and what might he say? Talking about problems and listening to what others say can sometimes help you to find solutions.

27

"What makes stepfamilies special?"

Children in stepfamilies often have a large number of relatives and family relationships. They learn to get along with a wide range of people – some of whom they like a lot and others they don't much care for.

Children who are part of a stepfamily learn, perhaps sooner than other children, how to ask for what they need from people around them. Many have lived through big changes in their lives and have adapted to these changes very well. Stepfamilies are experts on new beginnings and on making things work in a family group.

> When a baby is born , family members can share a special relationship with someone for whom this is the only family. Every member of the family will be special to the baby.

"What can I do?"

Living in a stepfamily is an experience lots of children share. If more people talk or write about them, or draw pictures of them, it would help more people to understand them and make them seem as ordinary as they are.

Many relatives are involved in making any one stepfamily work. Stepfamilies often have children who live in one home and visit another. The children of stepfamilies may have lived through their parents' separation or death. For all these reasons there are particular problems that can arise in stepfamilies. If you are living in a stepfamily and would like to talk to someone about it or receive some information, you can contact the organizations listed below.

Addresses for further information

Family Service America
333 7th Avenue
New York
N.Y. 10301

Help. Inc.
638 South Street
Philadelphia
Pennsylvania, 19147

What the words mean

divorce is the legal end of a marriage.

mourning is feeling sad about somebody you have lost or about a way of life you no longer have.

partner is a lover living with someone but not necessarily married.

relations or relatives are your parents, grandparents, brothers, sisters, cousins, aunts and uncles as well as stepparents, stepgrandparents, stepbrothers and stepsisters and other people who may be related to your family.

stepfamily is a family where one or both adult partners bring one or more children from the partnership they had before. The family may live together all the time, or only some of the time.

stepbrothers/stepsisters are the children of a parent's new partner.

stepparent is your father or mother's new partner.

Index

Photographic Credits:
Cover and pages 13, 17, 19, 21, 23 and 27: Marie-Helene
Bradley; pages 5, 9, 11, 15, 25 and 29: Timothy
Woodcock.

PRINTED IN BELGIUM BY
proost
INTERNATIONAL BOOK PRODUCTION